# Jetsology Trivia Challenge

## New York Jets Football

# Jetsology
# Trivia
# Challenge

## New York Jets Football

## Researched by Al Netzer

## Tom P. Rippey III & Paul F. Wilson, Editors

## Kick The Ball, Ltd
Lewis Center, Ohio

# Trivia by Kick The Ball, Ltd

## College Football Trivia

| | | | |
|---|---|---|---|
| Alabama Crimson Tide | Auburn Tigers | Boston College Eagles | Florida Gators |
| Georgia Bulldogs | LSU Tigers | Miami Hurricanes | Michigan Wolverines |
| Nebraska Cornhuskers | Notre Dame Fighting Irish | Ohio State Buckeyes | Oklahoma Sooners |
| Oregon Ducks | Penn State Nittany Lions | Southern Cal Trojans | Texas Longhorns |

## Pro Football Trivia

| | | | |
|---|---|---|---|
| Arizona Cardinals | Buffalo Bills | Chicago Bears | Cleveland Browns |
| Denver Broncos | Green Bay Packers | Indianapolis Colts | Kansas City Chiefs |
| Minnesota Vikings | New England Patriots | New Orleans Saints | New York Giants |
| New York Jets | Oakland Raiders | Philadelphia Eagles | Pittsburgh Steelers |
| San Francisco 49ers | Washington Redskins | | |

## Pro Baseball Trivia

| | | | |
|---|---|---|---|
| Boston Red Sox | Chicago Cubs | Chicago White Sox | Cincinnati Reds |
| Detroit Tigers | Los Angeles Dodgers | New York Mets | New York Yankees |
| Philadelphia Phillies | Saint Louis Cardinals | San Francisco Giants | |

## College Basketball Trivia

| | | | |
|---|---|---|---|
| Duke Blue Devils | Georgetown Hoyas | Indiana Hoosiers | Kansas Jayhawks |
| Kentucky Wildcats | Maryland Terrapins | Michigan State Spartans | North Carolina Tar Heels |
| Syracuse Orange | UConn Huskies | UCLA Bruins | |

## Pro Basketball Trivia

| | | | |
|---|---|---|---|
| Boston Celtics | Chicago Bulls | Detroit Pistons | Los Angeles Lakers |
| Utah Jazz | | | |

*This book is dedicated to our families and friends for your unwavering love, support, and your understanding of our pursuit of our passions. Thank you for everything you do for us and for making our lives complete.*

**Jetsology Trivia Challenge: New York Jets Football;**
**First Edition 2010**

Published by
Kick The Ball, Ltd
8595 Columbus Pike, Suite 197
Lewis Center, OH 43035
**www.TriviaGameBooks.com**

Designed, Formatted, and Edited by: Tom P. Rippey III and Paul F. Wilson
Researched by: Al Netzer

*For information on ordering this book in bulk at reduced prices, please email us at pfwilson@triviagamebooks.com.*

International Standard Book Number: 978-1-934372-85-2

Printed and Bound in the United States of America

10 9 8 7 6 5 4 3 2 1

# Table of Contents

Dear Friend,

Thank you for purchasing our *Jetsology Trivia Challenge* game book!

We have made every attempt to verify the accuracy of the questions and answers contained in this book. However it is still possible that from time to time an error has been made by us or our researchers. In the event you find a question or answer that is questionable or inaccurate, we ask for your understanding and thank you for bringing it to our attention so we may improve future editions of this book. Please email us at tprippey@triviagamebooks.com with those observations and comments.

Have fun playing *Jetsology Trivia Challenge*!

Tom & Paul

Tom Rippey & Paul Wilson
Co-Founders, Kick The Ball, Ltd

PS – You can discover more about all of our current trivia game books by visiting www.TriviaGameBooks.com.

**Book Format:**

There are four quarters, each made up of fifty questions. Each quarter's questions have assigned point values. Questions are designed to get progressively more difficult as you proceed through each quarter, as well as through the book itself. Most questions are in a four-option multiple-choice format so that you will at least have a 25% chance of getting a correct answer for some of the more challenging questions.

We have even added Overtime in the event of a tie, or just in case you want to keep playing a little longer.

**Game Options:**

**One Player -**
To play on your own, simply answer each of the questions in all the quarters, and in the overtime section, if you'd like. Use the Player / Team Score Sheet to record your answers and the quarter Answer Keys to check your answers. Calculate each quarter's points and the total for the game at the bottom of the Player / Team Score Sheet to determine your final score.

**Two or More Players –**
To play with multiple players decide if you will all be competing with each other individually, or if you will form and play as teams. Each player / team will then have its own Player / Team Score Sheet to record its answer. You can use the quarter Answer Keys to check your answers and to calculate your final scores.

The Player / Team Score Sheets have been designed so that each team can answer all questions or you can divide the questions up in any combination you would prefer. For example, you may want to alternate questions if two players are playing or answer every third question for three players, etc. In any case, simply record your response to your questions in the corresponding quarter and question number on the Player / Team Score Sheet.

A winner will be determined by multiplying the total number of correct answers for each quarter by the point value per quarter, then adding together the final total for all quarters combined. Play the game again and again by alternating the questions that your team is assigned so that you will answer a different set of questions each time you play.

**You Create the Game -**
There are countless other ways of using **Jetsology Trivia Challenge** questions. It is limited only to your imagination. Examples might be using them at your tailgate or other professional football related party. Players / Teams who answer questions incorrectly may have to perform a required action, or winners may receive special prizes. Let us know what other games you come up with!

Have fun!

1) What was the original nickname of the New York Jets' franchise?

Answers begin on page 17

A) Generals
B) Yankees
C) Titans
D) Knights

2) What are the New York Jets' team colors?

A) Green, Black, and White
B) Hunter Green and White
C) Green, Gray, Black, and White
D) Dark Navy, Old Gold, and White

3) What year did Giants Stadium open?

A) 1976
B) 1980
C) 1984
D) 1989

4) What year did New York play its first-ever game as the Jets?

A) 1961
B) 1963
C) 1964
D) 1967

5) With what team was Jets head coach Rex Ryans' first coaching job?

    A) Morehead State
    B) University of Cincinnati
    C) University of Oklahoma
    D) Eastern Kentucky

6) In which AFC Division does New York play?

    A) East
    B) South
    C) North
    D) West

7) What is the name of New York's team song?

    A) "Go! Jets! Go!"
    B) "We're the Jets"
    C) "The Jets Keep Sailing Along"
    D) "The Jets are Flying High"

8) How many times did the Jets play the College All-Stars?

    A) 1
    B) 2
    C) 3
    D) 5

9) How much did Jets quarterback Joe Namath sign for in 1965?

   A) $100,000
   B) $251,000
   C) $427,000
   D) $1,000,000

10) What is the name of the proposed new stadium for Jets football?

   A) New Meadowlands Stadium
   B) Jets-Giants Stadium
   C) Allianz Stadium
   D) Red Bull Arena

11) How much was the Jets' franchise purchased for in 1963?

   A) $675,000
   B) $750,000
   C) $897,000
   D) $1,000,000

12) Joe Namath was named the 1965 AFL Rookie of the Year.

   A) True
   B) False

13) What position did Jets coach Rex Ryan play in college?

    A) Linebacker
    B) Defensive End
    C) Tackle
    D) Center

14) Who was the first-ever player to sign a contract with the New York Titans?

    A) Art Powell
    B) Bill Mathis
    C) Don Maynard
    D) Dick Jamieson

15) Did Joe Namath start nine games for the Jets his rookie season?

    A) Yes
    B) No

16) When was the most recent season New York did not play a Monday Night Football (MNF) game?

    A) 1997
    B) 2001
    C) 2006
    D) 2007

17) How many years did the New York Jets call Shea Stadium home?

   A)  16
   B)  20
   C)  22
   D)  25

18) From which university have the Jets drafted the most players?

   A)  Penn State
   B)  Nebraska
   C)  Michigan
   D)  USC

19) Who holds New York's career rushing yards record?

   A)  Emerson Boozer
   B)  Matt Snell
   C)  Curtis Martin
   D)  Freeman McNeil

20) How many weeks were Jets players named NFL Rookie of the Week in 2009?

   A)  1
   B)  3
   C)  4
   D)  6

21) The New Meadowlands Stadium has a seating capacity over 65,000.

A) True
B) False

22) What year did New York's helmets change to all green with the Jets logo in a futuristic script?

A) 1964
B) 1967
C) 1971
D) 1978

23) Which New York head coach has the most career wins?

A) Bill Parcells
B) Walt Michaels
C) Weeb Ewbank
D) Herman Edwards

24) What year did Woody Johnson purchase the New York Jets from the estate of Leon Hess?

A) 1997
B) 2000
C) 2001
D) 2004

25) Who holds New York's record for passing yards in a single game?

   A)  Joe Namath
   B)  Ken O'Brien
   C)  Vinny Testaverde
   D)  Richard Todd

26) Which Jets player led the NFL in receiving yards in 1978?

   A)  Al Toon
   B)  Richard Caster
   C)  Bruce Harper
   D)  Wes Walker

27) How many times has New York played in the Super Bowl?

   A)  1
   B)  2
   C)  3
   D)  4

28) Where do the Jets hold their annual training camp?

   A)  Albany, N.Y.
   B)  Hempstead, N.Y.
   C)  Cortland, N.Y.
   D)  Bethlehem, Pa.

29) Have the Jets ever played the Giants in the postseason?

    A) Yes
    B) No

30) How many times has a Jet had greater than 1,000 kickoff return yards in a single season?

    A) 5
    B) 9
    C) 12
    D) 14

31) Who led the Jets in sacks during the 2009 regular season?

    A) David Harris
    B) Shaun Ellis
    C) Calvin Pace
    D) Jim Leonhard

32) Which team has New York played the most in postseason games?

    A) Oakland Raiders
    B) Indianapolis Colts
    C) Kansas City Chiefs
    D) San Diego Chargers

33) What are the most regular-season wins the Jets have ever had in a single season?

    A) 10
    B) 12
    C) 13
    D) 14

34) Which player holds the Jets' record for most all-purpose yards in a single season?

    A) Bruce Harper
    B) Curtis Martin
    C) Leon Washington
    D) Dick Christy

35) How many defensive touchdowns did the Jets have in 2009?

    A) 2
    B) 3
    C) 5
    D) 7

36) Who is the only Jet to gain 100 or more yards rushing and receiving in the same game?

    A) Bill Mathis
    B) Lamont Jordan
    C) Richie Anderson
    D) Johnny Hector

37) Who is the play-by-play announcer for the Jets Radio Network?

  A) Don La Greca
  B) Bob Wischusen
  C) Howard David
  D) Greg Buttle

38) Kellen Clemens had a better completion percentage in the Jets' 2009 regular season than Mark Sanchez.

  A) True
  B) False

39) In the lyrics of New York's fight song, what is the team supposed to fight like?

  A) Men
  B) Wild cats
  C) Titans
  D) Warriors

40) What is the name of the Jets' official airline?

  A) JetAmerica
  B) Continental Airlines
  C) ExpressJet Airlines
  D) JetBlue Airways

41) How many NFL opponents have never beaten the Jets at home?

    A) 3
    B) 4
    C) 5
    D) 7

42) Who holds New York's record for receiving yards in the regular season?

    A) Don Maynard
    B) George Saur
    C) Al Toon
    D) Laveranues Coles

43) Who holds the Jets' record for most passing yards in a rookie season?

    A) Ken O'Brien
    B) Joe Namath
    C) Mark Sanchez
    D) Richard Todd

44) When was the last time the Jets returned a blocked punt for a touchdown?

    A) 2001
    B) 2003
    C) 2007
    D) 2009

45) Which Jet holds the team's single-game rushing record?

    A) Curtis Martin
    B) Thomas Jones
    C) Emerson Boozer
    D) John Riggins

46) Who is the only Jet to be named Super Bowl MVP?

    A) Matt Snell
    B) George Sauer
    C) Emerson Boozer
    D) Joe Namath

47) How many Jets head coaches coached just one complete season?

    A) 2
    B) 3
    C) 5
    D) 6

48) Did the Jets score more points than they allowed during the 2009 regular season?

    A) Yes
    B) No

49) Who holds New York's record for points scored in a
career?

   A)  Jim Turner
   B)  Don Maynard
   C)  Pat Leahy
   D)  John Hall

50) What season did the Jets celebrate their first-ever
regular-season victory over the New York Giants?

   A)  1968
   B)  1974
   C)  1978
   D)  1981

NFL Draft day is filled with big names from big universities. Although Wayne Chrebet set many receiving records as a player at Hofstra University, he went undrafted in 1995. Eventually the Jets offered the 5'10", 188-pound receiver a chance to earn a roster spot as a walk-on. Upon his arrival on the first day of training camp, a Jets senior security guard stopped him at the gate, disbelieving that a player of his size had been invited to camp. Despite overwhelming odds, Chrebet made the team, working his way up from the bottom of the depth chart to become the team's receiving yards leader with 726 yards that season. An example of his resolve came in a game against Tampa Bay in 2000 when fellow teammate Keyshawn Johnson told the press that comparing Chrebet to him was like "comparing a flashlight to a star". Unshaken by the comment, Wayne caught a touchdown pass from Curtis Martin with 52 seconds remaining to win the game 21-17. Of Wayne's 580 career receptions, 379 came on successful third down conversions, earning him the nickname "Mr. Third Down". Wayne Chrebet retired in 2006 and his jersey number, 80, has yet to be reissued by the Jets.

1) C – Titans (The Titans were a founding member of the AFL in 1960.)

2) B – Hunter Green and White (These have been the Jets' official colors since 1998.)

3) A – 1976 (The Jets began playing their home games at Giants Stadium in 1984.)

4) B – 1963 (The Jets lost to the Patriots 14-38 on Sept. 8, 1963, at Boston College.)

5) D – Eastern Kentucky (Ryan was the defensive ends coach from 1987-88 with the Colonels of Eastern Kentucky.)

6) A – East (The Jets have played in the AFC East since 1970. They share the division with the Buffalo Bills, Miami Dolphins, and New England Patriots.)

7) C – "The Jets Keep Sailing Along" (This song was written by then-Jets coach Lou Holtz in 1976.)

8) A – 1 (The NFL Champion played the College All-Stars for 42 years from 1934-76. The Jets beat the College All-Stars 26-24 on Aug. 1, 1969.)

9) C – $427,000 (This was a record salary in 1965 when Namath chose to play for the Jets over the St. Louis Cardinals of the NFL. An added bonus was the new Lincoln Continental the Jets gave him.)

10) A – New Meadowlands Stadium (No naming rights deal had been reached as of the writing of this book.)

11) D – $1,000,000 (A group of five businessmen bought the team from Harry Wismer in 1963.)

12) A – True (Joe completed 164 passes on 340 attempts for 2,220 yards, 18 touchdowns, and 15 interceptions.)

13) B – Defensive End (Rex played alongside his twin brother Rob at Southwestern Oklahoma State University.)

14) C – Don Maynard (Don was a free agent, released by the New York Giants, when the Titans signed him in 1960.)

15) A – Yes (Joe had a record of 3-5-1 in the nine games he started for the Jets in 1965.)

16) D – 2007 (This was the only year in the 2000s that the Jets did not play a Monday Night Football game.)

17) B – 20 (The Jets played their home games in Shea Stadium from 1964-83.)

18) A – Penn State (The Jets have drafted 18 players from Penn State. The most recent was OT Kareem McKenzie, the 17th pick in the third round of the 2001 NFL Draft.)

19) C – Curtis Martin (He gained 10,302 yards rushing on 2,560 attempts from 1998-2005.)

20) B – 3 (Mark Sanchez was named Rookie of the Week for the first three weeks of 2009.)

21) A – True (Official seating capacity is 82,500.)

22) D – 1978 (The Jets changed both their helmets and uniform design in 1978.)

23) C – Weeb Ewbank (71 wins from 1963-73)

24) B – 2000 (Johnson won a bidding war for the team with a purchase price of $635 million.)

25) A – Joe Namath (Joe completed 15 of 28 passes for 496 yards against the Baltimore Colts in 1972.)

26) D – Wes Walker (Wes recorded 1,169 yards on 48 catches with eight touchdowns.)

27) A – 1 (Super Bowl III in 1969)

28) C – Cortland, N.Y. (Since 2009 the Jets have trained at the State University of New York College in Cortland, N.Y.)

29) B – No (The Jets and Giants have only been in the playoffs the same year on five occasions.)

30) B – 9 (Four Jets have had over 1,000 kickoff return yards in a season nine times, the most recent was Leon Washington in 2008 with 1,231 yards on 48 returns.)

31) C – Calvin Pace (Calvin recorded eight sacks in 12 games.)

32) A – Oakland Raiders (The Jets have played the Raiders four times in the postseason, going 2-2 in those games.)

33) B – 12 (The Jets won 12 games during the regular season in 1998.)

34) C – Leon Washington (Leon recorded 2,337 all-purpose yards in 2008, which led the NFL and set the team's single-season record.)

35) A – 2 (Darrelle Revis had a 67-yard interception return for a touchdown against the Panthers in Week 12 and Marques Douglas had a 1-yard fumble return touchdown against the Colts in Week 16.)

36) D – Johnny Hector (Johnny had 117 rushing yards and 100 receiving yards against the Bills in 1986.)

37) B – Bob Wischusen (Bob has been the play-by-play voice of the Jets since 2002.)

38) B – False (Kellen completed 13 of 26 passes for .500 while Mark was 196 of 364 for .538.)

39) A – Men (The first line in the Jets fight song is "Win the game, fight like men".)

40) D – JetBlue Airways (New York's JetBlue signed a three-year deal in 2009 to become the Jets' official airline.)

41) C – 5 (The Jets are undefeated at home against the Buccaneers [6-0], Packers [4-0], Panthers [2-0], Texans [2-0], and Vikings [4-0].)

42) A – Don Maynard (In 1967, Don gained 1,434 yards in 14 games.)

43) C – Mark Sanchez (Mark recorded 2,444 passing yards with 12 touchdowns in 2009.)

44) D – 2009 (Eric Smith blocked the punt of New England's Chris Hanson. Brad Smith picked it up at the 4-yard line and ran it in for a Jets touchdown.)

45) B – Thomas Jones (Jones rushed for a franchise-record 210 yards against the Buffalo Bills on Oct. 18, 2009.)

46) D – Joe Namath (Joe won the award in Super Bowl III by leading the Jets to a victory over the Baltimore Colts. He completed 17 of 28 passes for 206 yards with no touchdowns or interceptions.)

47) B – 3 (Bulldog Turner [1962], Pete Carroll [1994], and Al Groh [2000])

48) A – Yes (The Jets scored 348 points and allowed only 236.)

49) C – Pat Leahy (1,470 career points scored from 1974-91 [304 field goals, 558 points after touchdowns])

50) B – 1974 (The Jets beat the Giants 26-20 in overtime on Nov. 10, 1974, at the Yale Bowl.)

Note: All answers valid as of the end of the 2009 season, unless otherwise indicated in the question itself.

1) What is the Jets' team record for most total yards in a single game?

Answers begin on page 37

   A)  517
   B)  556
   C)  581
   D)  597

2) What jersey number did the Jets' Joe Klecko wear?

   A)  57
   B)  68
   C)  73
   D)  77

3) When was the last time the Jets drafted a running back in the first round?

   A)  1987
   B)  1990
   C)  2000
   D)  2003

4) Which decade did New York have the highest winning percentage?

   A)  1960s
   B)  1980s
   C)  1990s
   D)  2000s

5) What are the most rushing yards by the Jets in a postseason game?

    A)  196
    B)  210
    C)  234
    D)  257

6) What is New York's record for most consecutive 10-win seasons?

    A)  2
    B)  3
    C)  4
    D)  5

7) Does New York have an all-time winning record against the Dolphins?

    A)  Yes
    B)  No

8) Where did Rex Ryan serve as assistant head coach before becoming the Jets head coach?

    A)  Cincinnati Bengals
    B)  Philadelphia Eagles
    C)  Atlanta Falcons
    D)  Baltimore Ravens

9) Who holds the Jets' record for most games in a season with 300 or more passing yards?

A) Ken O'Brien
B) Joe Namath
C) Vinny Testaverde
D) Richard Todd

10) Do the Jets have an all-time winning record in games following a bye week?

A) Yes
B) No

11) What are the most points the Jets ever allowed in a postseason game?

A) 31
B) 34
C) 38
D) 42

12) How many teams has New York played 50 or more times in the regular season?

A) 4
B) 5
C) 7
D) 8

13) Does New York's Kellen Clemens have greater than 500 career passing attempts?

    A)  Yes
    B)  No

14) Who was the most recent player to gain greater than 200 yards rushing against New York?

    A)  Cedric Benson
    B)  Edgerrin James
    C)  Clinton Portis
    D)  Thurman Thomas

15) What is the Giants Stadium record for longest field goal kicked by a Jet?

    A)  51 yards
    B)  53 yards
    C)  55 yards
    D)  57 yards

16) Who was the most recent Jet to lead the NFL in receptions?

    A)  Al Toon
    B)  Laveranues Coles
    C)  Jerricho Cotchery
    D)  Keyshawn Johnson

17) Against which team was New York's first-ever NFL win?

    A) Denver Broncos
    B) Buffalo Bills
    C) Houston Oilers
    D) Dallas Texans

18) When was the last time the Jets had over 500 yards of total offense in a postseason game?

    A) 1983
    B) 1991
    C) 1999
    D) 2009

19) How many times has New York had the No. 1 overall draft pick?

    A) 1
    B) 2
    C) 4
    D) 5

20) His job at New York is Rex Ryan's first head coaching position at any level.

    A) True
    B) False

21) How many yards is the longest rushing play in New York history?

    A)  79
    B)  83
    C)  90
    D)  97

22) How many teams has New York never beaten at home?

    A)  1
    B)  2
    C)  4
    D)  5

23) What is the Jets' record for most rushing yards in a single game?

    A)  263
    B)  287
    C)  302
    D)  333

24) How many times has New York played in the AFC Wild Card Playoff Game?

    A)  6
    B)  8
    C)  10
    D)  11

25) The Jets were outgained in their only Super Bowl appearance.

    A) True
    B) False

26) What year did the Jets win their first-ever postseason game?

    A) 1963
    B) 1966
    C) 1967
    D) 1968

27) How many times has New York lost a season opener played at home?

    A) 19
    B) 24
    C) 28
    D) 31

28) How many New York players have been named AP NFL Defensive Rookie of the Year?

    A) 1
    B) 3
    C) 4
    D) 5

29) How many years did Pat Leahy play football for the Jets?

  A)  12
  B)  13
  C)  15
  D)  18

30) How many regular-season games did New York play in its first-ever AFL season?

  A)  10
  B)  12
  C)  14
  D)  16

31) Who was the Jets' opponent on the first-ever Monday Night Football broadcast in 1970?

  A)  Buffalo Bills
  B)  Miami Dolphins
  C)  Minnesota Vikings
  D)  Cleveland Browns

32) Do the Jets have an all-time winning record against the NFC?

  A)  Yes
  B)  No

33) Who was the most recent Jet to have over 90 receptions in a single season?

    A) Laveranues Coles
    B) Keyshawn Johnson
    C) Santana Moss
    D) Richie Anderson

34) Who is the only Jet to have greater than 225 receiving yards in a single game?

    A) Al Toon
    B) Wes Walker
    C) Don Maynard
    D) Rich Castor

35) To which team did New York suffer its biggest loss in its first NFL season?

    A) Los Angeles Chargers
    B) Boston Patriots
    C) Houston Oilers
    D) Oakland Raiders

36) Who was New York's first-ever opponent at Giants Stadium?

    A) Indianapolis Colts
    B) Buffalo Bills
    C) Miami Dolphins
    D) Pittsburgh Steelers

37) How many yards was the Jets' longest touchdown drive in 2009?

   A) 81
   B) 85
   C) 93
   D) 97

38) What are the most Pro Bowl appearances by a New York Jet?

   A) 3
   B) 5
   C) 7
   D) 9

39) Who holds New York's record for passing yards in a season?

   A) Joe Namath
   B) Boomer Esiason
   C) Ken O'Brien
   D) Brett Favre

40) In 2009 the Jets led the NFL in both rushing offense and rushing defense.

   A) True
   B) False

41) Who holds New York's record for most receptions in a single regular-season game?

   A)  Al Toon
   B)  Jerricho Cotchery
   C)  Clark Gaines
   D)  Santana Moss

42) How many quarterbacks started just one game for the New York Jets?

   A)  3
   B)  5
   C)  6
   D)  8

43) When was the last time the Jets had a punt blocked?

   A)  2000
   B)  2002
   C)  2006
   D)  2008

44) Since 2001, who holds the Jets' record for most career tackles?

   A)  Eric Barton
   B)  Jonathan Vilma
   C)  Kerry Rhodes
   D)  David Harris

45) Did Joe Namath have greater than 30,000 career passing yards?

    A) Yes
    B) No

46) Who holds the Jets' record for career sacks?

    A) Mark Gastineau
    B) Shaun Ellis
    C) Joe Klecko
    D) Marty Lyons

47) How many Jets had over 1,250 yards receiving in a single season?

    A) 1
    B) 2
    C) 5
    D) 7

48) How many New York head coaches have been named NFL Coach of the Year?

    A) 1
    B) 2
    C) 3
    D) 4

49) How many times have the Jets scored an average of 25 or more points per game in a season?

A) 5
B) 6
C) 8
D) 10

50) How many times has a Jet been awarded the Walter Payton NFL Man of The Year Award?

A) 1
B) 2
C) 3
D) 4

Of all the games played on Monday Night Football, one of the most memorable for Jets fans took place between the Jets and Dolphins in 2000. It has been called "The Monday Night Miracle" and set a Jets record for largest-ever fourth quarter comeback. After a dismal three quarters of play by the Jets, the Dolphins led 30-7 to start the fourth. Jets radio announcer Howard David remarked, "And with a whole quarter to go, this game is over." However, the Jets never quit. Miami's Sam Madison bobbled an almost certain interception early in the fourth, instead, Laveranues Coles caught the pass for a touchdown. Let the comeback begin. Vinny Testaverde threw three more touchdown passes in the fourth quarter. The most memorable was his last. Jets offensive tackle Jumbo Elliott caught a three-yard touchdown pass, the first of his career, to tie the game 37-37 with 1:20 left to play. In overtime, New York's John Hall kicked a 40-yard field goal to complete the comeback and to win the game 40-37. In 2009, NFL.com listed the game at number five on its list of Top Ten Comebacks of All-Time.

1) D – 597 (The Jets had 171 rushing yards and 426 passing yards against the Dolphins in 1988.)

2) C – 73 (Klecko played defensive end and tackle for the Jets from 1977-87.)

3) B – 1990 (The Jets drafted Blair Thomas from Penn State with the second pick of the 1990 NFL Draft.)

4) A – 1960s (The Jets went 69-65-6, for a .514 winning percentage.)

5) C – 234 (In the 1982 AFC Wild Card game, the Jets rushed for 234 yards and limited the Bengals to just 62 yards on the ground.)

6) A – 2 (The Jets have had two consecutive 10-win seasons twice in their history, back-to-back in 1968 [11-3] and 1969 [10-4], and again in 1985 [11-5] and 1986 [10-6].)

7) A – Yes (NY is 46-43-1 [.517] all-time vs. the Dolphins.)

8) D – Baltimore Ravens (Rex served under John Harbaugh as assistant head coach in 2008.)

9) B – Joe Namath (Joe passed for greater than 300 yards in a game six times in 1967.)

10) A – Yes (The Jets are 11-10 [.524] in games after a bye week since the NFL began using them in 1990.)

11) C – 38 (The Jets lost 24-38 to the Raiders in the 2002 AFC Wild Card game.)

12) A – 4 (Bills [98], Patriots [98], Dolphins [88], and Colts [68])

13) B – No (Kellen has attempted 282 passes in 24 games since being drafted by the Jets in the 2006 draft.)

14) D – Thurman Thomas (In 1990, Buffalo running back Thurman Thomas gained 214 yards on 18 carries against the Jets.)

15) C – 55 yards (This record is shared by Pat Leahy, against Chicago in 1985, and Jay Feely, against St. Louis in 2008 and Miami in 2009.)

16) A – Al Toon (Al led the league in 1988 with 93 receptions in 15 games.)

17) B – Buffalo Bills (The Titans beat the Bills 27-3 at the Polo Grounds in 1960.)

18) A – 1983 (The Jets gained 517 yards in a 44-17 win against the Bengals in the 1983 AFC Wild Card game [234 yards rushing and 283 yards passing].)

19) B – 2 (The Jets selected Joe Namath No. 1 overall in the 1965 AFL Draft and Keyshawn Johnson No. 1 overall in the 1996 NFL Draft.)

20) A – True (Rex was assistant head coach with two teams [Baltimore Ravens and New Mexico Highlands] as well as being defensive coordinator with several other teams.)

21) C – 90 (Johnny Johnson set this record against the Bears in 1994.)

22) B – 2 (The Jets are 0-4 at home against both the Philadelphia Eagles and the Washington Redskins.)

23) D – 333 (John Riggins [168], Emerson Boozer [150], Steve Harkey [10], and Cliff McClain [5] combined for 333 yards against the Patriots in 1972.)

24) C – 10 (The Jets are 5-5 all-time in AFC Wild Card Playoff games [1981, 1982, 1985, 1986, 1991, 2001, 2002, 2004, 2006, and 2009].)

25) B – False (The Jets had 337 total yards [195 passing and 142 rushing] to the Colts' 324 total yards [181 passing and 143 rushing].)

26) D – 1968 (The Jets beat the Raiders 27-23 in the 1968 AFL Championship Game.)

27) C – 28 (The Jets are 22-28 [.440] in home openers.)

28) B – 3 (Eric McMillan [1988], Hugh Douglas [1995], and Jonathan Vilma [2004])

29) D – 18 (Pat holds the longevity record for the Jets. He was Jets kicker from 1974-91.)

30) C – 14 (The Jets were 7-7 their first-ever season.)

31) D – Cleveland Browns (The Jets lost 21-31 to the Browns at Cleveland Stadium in the very first Monday Night Football broadcast.)

32) B – No (The Jets have an all-time record of 69-88 [.439] against NFC teams.)

33) A – Laveranues Coles (Coles caught 91 passes for 1,098 yards and six touchdowns in 2006.)

34) C – Don Maynard (He gained 228 yards on 10 receptions against the Raiders in 1968.)

35) B – Boston Patriots (The New York Titans lost 21-38 to the Boston Patriots, who in 1971 would become the New England Patriots.)

36) D – Pittsburgh Steelers (The Jets lost 17-23 to the Steelers in the second game of 1984.)

37) C – 93 (The Jets had a 93-yard touchdown drive in the second quarter against the Oakland Raiders on Oct. 25, 2009.)

38) B – 5 (Two players for the Jets have played in five Pro Bowls each, Mark Gastineau [1981-85] and Kevin Mawae [1999-03].)

39) A – Joe Namath (Joe passed for 4,007 yards in 14 games in 1967. He was the first QB in history to pass for 4,000 yards in a single season.)

40) B – False (The Jets led the NFL in rushing offense [2,756 yards] but were eighth in rushing defense [1,578 yards].)

41) C – Clark Gaines (He had 17 receptions for 160 yards from Richard Todd against the 49ers in 1980.)

42) A – 3 (Dick Jamieson [1960], J.J. Jones [1975], and Kyle Mackey [1989])

43) D – 2008 (Miami's Charlie Anderson blocked a Reggie Hodges punt on Dec. 28, 2008.)

44) C – Kerry Rhodes (Kerry has 327 career tackles from 2005-09. Tackles did not become an official NFL statistic until 2001.)

45) B – No (Joe passed for 27,663 yards in his career [27,057 yards as a Jet].)

46) A – Mark Gastineau (Mark recorded 107.5 sacks for his career with the Jets from 1979-88 [74 official sacks from 1982-88]. Sacks did not become an official NFL statistic until 1982.)

47) B – 2 (Don Maynard in 1967 [1,434 yards], 1968 [1,297 yards], and 1960 [1,265 yards] and Laveranues Coles in 2002 [1,264 yards])

48) A – 1 (UPI named Walt Michaels NFL Coach of the Year in 1978.)

49) C – 8 (1960 [27.3 points per game], 1967 [26.5 ppg], 1968 [29.9 ppg], 1969 [25.2 ppg], 1972 [26.2 ppg], 1982 [27.2 ppg], 1998 [26.0 ppg], and 2008 [25.3 ppg])

50) B – 2 (The Walter Payton Award was given to Marty Lyons [1984] and Boomer Esiason [1995]. This award honors a player's charity work, as well as his performance on the field.)

Note: All answers valid as of the end of the 2009 season, unless otherwise indicated in the question itself.

1) How many times has New York lost in the AFC Championship game?

Answers begin on page 56

    A)  1
    B)  3
    C)  4
    D)  6

2) How many times have the Jets played on Thanksgiving Day?

    A)  3
    B)  4
    C)  6
    D)  9

3) Which year was New York's first-ever 10-win season?

    A)  1968
    B)  1969
    C)  1974
    D)  1981

4) Which Jets head coach has the second most wins while at New York?

    A)  Walt Michaels
    B)  Joe Walton
    C)  Herman Edwards
    D)  Bruce Coslet

5) What is New York's largest margin of victory in a postseason game?

  A)  24 points
  B)  27 points
  C)  35 points
  D)  41 points

6) Who holds the Jets' career record for receiving yards?

  A)  Don Maynard
  B)  Al Toon
  C)  Wayne Chrebet
  D)  Wes Walker

7) Which of the following New York quarterbacks never threw five touchdown passes in a single game?

  A)  Joe Namath
  B)  Brett Favre
  C)  Boomer Esiason
  D)  Neil O'Donnell

8) How many combined kickoffs and punts were returned for touchdowns by the Jets in 2009?

  A)  1
  B)  3
  C)  4
  D)  5

9) What is New York's record for points after touchdown (PATs) made in a single game?

A) 4
B) 5
C) 7
D) 8

10) What is the only decade the Jets failed to have a 10-win season?

A) 1960s
B) 1970s
C) 1980s
D) 1990s

11) Freeman McNeil played in the most postseason games as a Jet.

A) True
B) False

12) How many combined career 300-yard passing games did Jet quarterbacks Joe Namath and Ken O'Brien have?

A) 28
B) 33
C) 38
D) 45

13) How many times has a rookie led the Jets in sacks?

    A)  2
    B)  4
    C)  5
    D)  7

14) Who is the only Jets defender to record twelve or more interceptions in a single season?

    A)  Burgess Owens
    B)  Erik McMillan
    C)  Darrelle Revis
    D)  Dainard Paulson

15) Which Jets coach has the highest career regular-season winning percentage?

    A)  Bill Parcells
    B)  Rex Ryan
    C)  Al Groh
    D)  Sammy Baugh

16) How many New York quarterbacks have started 50 or more games?

    A)  3
    B)  5
    C)  6
    D)  8

17) Who was the most recent Jet to record greater than 150 total defensive tackles in a single season?

   A)  Eric Barton
   B)  Sam Cowart
   C)  Kerry Rhodes
   D)  Jonathan Vilma

18) What is the Jets' all-time record for most consecutive losses?

   A)  9 games
   B)  10 games
   C)  12 games
   D)  16 games

19) When was the only time the season-leading passer for New York had fewer than 1,000 yards passing?

   A)  1960
   B)  1971
   C)  1984
   D)  1999

20) Who was the most recent receiver to lead the Jets in scoring?

   A)  Rich Caster
   B)  Art Powell
   C)  Don Maynard
   D)  Wes Walker

21) What is New York's all-time winning percentage at home (regular season and postseason)?

    A)  .489
    B)  .503
    C)  .521
    D)  .557

22) Do the Jets have official team cheerleaders?

    A)  Yes
    B)  No

23) Who was the most recent Jet to have his jersey number retired?

    A)  Joe Namath
    B)  Don Maynard
    C)  Mark Gastineau
    D)  Joe Klecko

24) How many seasons have the Jets gained greater than 2,500 rushing yards as a team?

    A)  1
    B)  2
    C)  4
    D)  5

25) Jet Gerry Philbin was named to the American Football League All-Time Team.

    A) True
    B) False

26) Which team did the Jets play in their only overtime game of 2009?

    A) Jacksonville Jaguars
    B) Miami Dolphins
    C) Buffalo Bills
    D) Atlanta Falcons

27) Who is the only New York running back to be named AFL Rookie of the Year?

    A) Emerson Boozer
    B) Matt Snell
    C) John Riggins
    D) Freeman McNeil

28) All-time, how many seasons have non-kickers led the Jets in scoring?

    A) 1
    B) 3
    C) 4
    D) 8

29) Which year did New York get its 300th all-time regular-season win?

A)  1998
B)  2001
C)  2003
D)  2004

30) What is the combined winning percentage for Jets head coaches who lasted one season or less?

A)  .369
B)  .411
C)  .497
D)  .515

31) How many times in regular-season games did a Jets running back rush for greater than 100 yards in 2009?

A)  4
B)  7
C)  8
D)  10

32) What is New York's longest drought between playoff appearances?

A)  7 years
B)  9 years
C)  11 years
D)  14 years

33) Against which NFC team does New York have the highest all-time winning percentage (min. 3 games)?

A) Green Bay Packers
B) Detroit Lions
C) Tampa Bay Buccaneers
D) Arizona Cardinals

34) How did New York score its first points in Super Bowl III?

A) Safety
B) Touchdown Pass
C) Field Goal
D) Touchdown Run

35) Has New York ever failed to rush for 1,000 yards as a team in a season?

A) Yes
B) No

36) How many consecutive Jets games did Kyle Clifton play?

A) 187
B) 198
C) 204
D) 216

37) Who was the Jets' first round pick in the 2010 NFL Draft?

   A) Joe McKnight
   B) Kyle Wilson
   C) Vladimir Ducasse
   D) John Conner

38) Who is the only player to lead New York in passing and rushing yards in the same year?

   A) Al Dorow
   B) Dick Wood
   C) John Green
   D) Dick Christy

39) Which Jets player intercepted two passes in Super Bowl III?

   A) John Dockery
   B) Cornell Gordon
   C) Johnny Sample
   D) Randy Beverly

40) When was the most recent season the leading rusher for New York gained fewer than 500 yards?

   A) 1963
   B) 1967
   C) 1983
   D) 1990

41) When was the last time the Jets went undefeated in the preseason?

   A) 1996
   B) 1999
   C) 2002
   D) 2005

42) What is New York's all-time record for largest margin of victory?

   A) 39 points
   B) 44 points
   C) 47 points
   D) 54 points

43) In which state did New York hold its training camp in 1960?

   A) New Jersey
   B) Connecticut
   C) Pennsylvania
   D) New Hampshire

44) Who coached New York immediately after Bruce Coslet?

   A) Pete Carroll
   B) Eric Mangini
   C) Lou Holtz
   D) Al Groh

45) Who scored the first touchdowns for the Jets in the 2009 AFC Wild Card game versus the Bengals?

    A) Thomas Jones
    B) Mark Sanchez
    C) Shonn Greene
    D) Brad Smith

46) Did Eric Mangini win his final game as the Jets head coach?

    A) Yes
    B) No

47) How many interceptions did the Jets defense have in 2009?

    A) 8
    B) 10
    C) 13
    D) 17

48) How many New York receivers had 50 or more receptions in the 2009 regular season?

    A) 1
    B) 2
    C) 3
    D) 4

49) When was the most recent season New York led the NFL in total tackles?

    A)  1996
    B)  2001
    C)  2005
    D)  2008

50) What is New York's all-time record for most consecutive playoff losses?

    A)  2
    B)  3
    C)  5
    D)  6

According to a Texas football legend, the former coach of Texas A&M pulled into a small town gas station and found a punter who would become an All-American, a future Jets draft pick, and an NFL record holder. The coach was Gene Stallings. The gas station owner told him about Steve O'Neal, who was enrolled at A&M on a track scholarship. Steve was a punter on his high school team, but so was the coach's son. He became the full-time punter his senior year when the coach's son was injured. At A&M, he was given a tryout and quickly made the team. His 41.8-yard career punting average still ranks fourth at Texas A&M. Drafted by the Jets in the 13th round in 1969, Steve had a great training camp and found himself starting for the defending Super Bowl Champions that year. It was in the second game of the 1969 season, against the Broncos, that Steve set the NFL record with a 98-yard punt. The Jets were at their one-yard line when O'Neal booted his record-setting punt. The football flew out of the end zone, over the head of the return man, hit the Broncos' 35-yard line, and started bouncing toward the goal line. When the Broncos player picked it up, the Jets tackled him at the one-yard line. The result was a 98-yard punt that still stands alone as an NFL record.

1) B – 3 (The Jets lost to the Dolphins in 1982 [0-14], the Broncos in 1998 [10-23], and the Colts in 2009 [17-30].)

2) C – 6 (The Jets are 3-3 all-time in Thanksgiving Day games. Their most recent appearance was a loss to the Dallas Cowboys [3-34] on Nov. 22, 2007.)

3) A – 1968 (The Jets went 11-3, finishing the season as Super Bowl Champions.)

4) B – Joe Walton (Joe coached the Jets to a 53-57-1 [.482] record from 1983-89.)

5) D – 41 points (The Jets beat the Colts 41-0 in the AFC Wild Card game on Jan. 4, 2003.)

6) A – Don Maynard (Don gained 11,732 receiving yards from 1960-72.)

7) C – Boomer Esiason (The most he ever threw in a single game as a Jet were four touchdown passes. He did this once against the Eagles in 1993.)

8) A – 1 (One kickoff return for a touchdown was recorded by Brad Smith in a game against the Colts on Dec. 27, 2009. Brad set the Jets' record for longest kickoff return at 106 yards.)

9) D – 8 (Pat Leahy completed all eight attempts in a 62-28 win against the Buccaneers in 1985.)

10) B – 1970s (The most wins the Jets had in a season during the 1970s were eight in 1978 and 1979.)

11) A – True (He played in eight postseason games as a Jet; one in 1981, 1985, and 1991; two in 1986; and three in 1982.)

12) C – 38 (Joe [21 300-yard games] and Ken [17 300-yard games] make up almost half of the 78 total all-time 300-yard passing games in Jets history.)

13) B – 4 (Alex Gordon [5 sacks in 1987], Dennis Byrd [7 sacks in 1989], Hugh Douglas [10 sacks in 1995], and David Harris [5 sacks in 2007])

14) D – Dainard Paulson (In 1964, he led the AFL with 12 interceptions.)

15) A – Bill Parcells (He was 29-19 for a .604 winning percentage from 1997-99.)

16) B – 5 (Joe Namath [126], Ken O'Brien [106], Richard Todd [93], Chad Pennington [61], and Vinny Testaverde [61])

17) D – Jonathan Vilma (He recorded 173 total tackles in 2005 [128 solo and 45 assisted].)

18) C – 12 games (The Jets lost 12 straight games from Dec. 3, 1995 to Oct. 20, 1996.)

19) B – 1971 (Bob Davis led the team with 624 yards passing [49 completions on 121 attempts].)

20) A – Rich Caster (In 1974, TE Rich Caster tied RB John Riggins with 42 points each [7 touchdowns] to lead the Jets in scoring.)

21) C – .521 (NY has a 190-178-5 all-time home record.)

22) A – Yes (The Jets' official cheerleaders are called the Jets Flight Crew, they began in 2006 as the Jets Flag Crew.)

23) D – Joe Klecko (The Jets retired Joe Klecko's jersey number 73 during a halftime ceremony in a game against the New England Patriots on Dec. 26, 2004.)

24) B – 2 (1979 [2,646 yards] and 2009 [2,756 yards])

25) A – True (Gerry Philbin was a DE for the Jets from 1964-72. The AFL All-Time Team was voted on in 1970 by a panel of football writers from AFL team cities.)

26) C – Buffalo Bills (New York lost the game when the Bills' Rian Lindell kicked a 47-yard field goal with 2:49 left in overtime.)

27) B – Matt Snell (Matt recorded 948 rushing yards, 393 receiving yards, 158 kickoff return yards, and was named 1964 AFL Rookie of the Year.)

28) B – 3 (Bill Mathis and Don Maynard [1961], Rich Caster and John Riggins [1974], and Kevin Long [1979])

29) D – 2004 (The Jets beat the Dolphins 41-14 in the seventh game of the 2004 season to record their 300th all-time win.)

30) A – .369 (One-season Jets head coaches had a combined record of 24-41.)

31) C – 8 (Thomas Jones [7] and Shonn Greene [1])

32) D – 11 years (The Jets failed to make the playoffs from 1970-80.)

33) C – Tampa Bay Buccaneers (The Jets have an all-time winning percentage of .900 [9-1] against Tampa Bay.)

34) D – Touchdown Run (Matt Snell ran off left tackle for a four-yard touchdown, capping an 80-yard drive in the second quarter.)

35) A – Yes (In 1963 the Jets rushed for 978 yards. It was the only season they had under 1,000 yards in team history.)

36) C – 204 (Kyle played linebacker for the Jets from 1984-96.)

37) B – Kyle Wilson (New York drafted cornerback Kyle Wilson out of Boise State with the 29th pick of the 2010 NFL Draft.)

38) A – Al Dorow (In 1960, Al recorded 2,748 passing yards and 453 rushing yards to lead the Titans in both categories.)

39) D – Randy Beverly (Randy was the first player to record two interceptions in a Super Bowl, both coming in the end zone. He played for the Jets from 1967-69.)

40) B – 1967 (Emerson Boozer led the Jets with 442 yards on 119 carries and 10 touchdowns.)

41) C – 2002 (The Jets defeated the Steelers [16-6], Ravens [34-16], Giants [28-7], and Eagles [23-16].)

42) B – 44 points (The Jets beat the St. Louis Rams 47-3 on Nov. 9, 2008.)

43) D – New Hampshire (The Titans held their training camp at the University of New Hampshire in 1960.)

44) A – Pete Carroll (Bruce was fired after the Jets went 8-8 in 1993. Pete Carroll was elevated from defensive coordinator to head coach for the 1994 season.)

45) C – Shonn Greene (Shonn ran for a 39-yard touchdown and Jay Feely's PAT tied the score [7-7] early in the second quarter.)

46) B – No (Mangini's Jets lost to the Dolphins 17-24 to finish the season with a 9-7 record.)

47) D – 17 (The Jets' 17 interceptions totaled 247 yards and one touchdown.)

48) A – 1 (Jerricho Cotchery led all Jets receivers with 57 receptions in 14 games.)

49) D – 2008 (The Jets recorded 1,197 total tackles [886 solo and 311 assisted] to lead the NFL in total tackles.)

50) A – 2 (New York lost two playoff games in a row five times [1969 and 1981, 1982 and 1985, 1986 and 1991, 1998 and 2001, and then in 2004 and 2006])

Note: All answers valid as of the end of the 2009 season, unless otherwise indicated in the question itself.

## Jetsology Trivia Challenge

1) When was the most recent season a Jets game resulted in a tie?

Answers begin on page 75

    A)  1977
    B)  1988
    C)  1994
    D)  1999

2) Which opponent handed New York its largest defeat in 2009?

    A)  Jacksonville Jaguars
    B)  Miami Dolphins
    C)  New Orleans Saints
    D)  New England Patriots

3) How many Jets have their jersey number retired?

    A)  2
    B)  3
    C)  5
    D)  6

4) Has a Jets running back ever had five rushing touchdowns in a single game?

    A)  Yes
    B)  No

5) Which player holds New York's record for most consecutive field goals made?

    A)   Jay Feely
    B)   Mike Nugent
    C)   Pat Leahy
    D)   John Hall

6) Who was the most recent head coach to win his first regular-season game with New York?

    A)   Bill Parcells
    B)   Herman Edwards
    C)   Rex Ryan
    D)   Al Groh

7) What is New York's record for most consecutive years appearing in the postseason?

    A)   2
    B)   3
    C)   5
    D)   6

8) Which New York head coach is in the Pro Football Hall of Fame?

    A)   Herman Edwards
    B)   Joe Walton
    C)   Walt Michaels
    D)   Weeb Ewbank

9) Against which NFC team does New York have the largest all-time winning percentage (min. 3 games)?

A) Dallas Cowboys
B) Washington Redskins
C) San Francisco 49ers
D) Philadelphia Eagles

10) Did Bill Parcells coach the New England Patriots prior to coaching the New York Jets?

A) Yes
B) No

11) Which of the following Jets players was not named a First-team All-Pro in 1968?

A) Gerry Philbin
B) Joe Namath
C) Don Maynard
D) George Sauer

12) When was the last season a Jets defender had three interceptions in the same game?

A) 1994
B) 1998
C) 2000
D) 2005

13) In which of the following categories did the Jets' Curtis Martin not lead the NFL in 2004?

A) Rushing Touchdowns
B) Rushing Attempts
C) Touches
D) Rushing Yards

14) Who holds New York's record for most punting yards in a single season?

A) Steve Weatherford
B) Brian Hansen
C) Tom Tupa
D) Chuck Ramsey

15) When was the last time the Jets were shut out?

A) 1997
B) 2000
C) 2003
D) 2006

16) Brett Favre led the NFL in interceptions when he played for New York in 2008.

A) True
B) False

17) How many times has a Jets player led the NFL in non-offensive touchdowns?

    A) 4
    B) 5
    C) 8
    D) 10

18) When was the most recent season the Jets had two receivers with greater than 1,000 yards receiving?

    A) 1986
    B) 1998
    C) 2002
    D) 2007

19) Who holds New York's record for most consecutive games with a full sack?

    A) Joe Klecko
    B) John Abraham
    C) Shaun Ellis
    D) Mark Gastineau

20) Which New York quarterback holds the team record for highest passer rating in a single season?

    A) Joe Namath
    B) Ken O'Brien
    C) Vinny Testaverde
    D) Chad Pennington

21) How many total head coaches have the Jets had in their history?

    A)   15
    B)   17
    C)   20
    D)   22

22) What is New York's largest margin of victory over the Miami Dolphins?

    A)   21 points
    B)   24 points
    C)   27 points
    D)   33 points

23) Which Jets head coach has the second highest regular-season winning percentage at New York (min. 3 seasons)?

    A)   Eric Mangini
    B)   Joe Walton
    C)   Weeb Ewbank
    D)   Herman Edwards

24) Has New York played every NFL team at least once?

    A)   Yes
    B)   No

25) Which Jet won the Ed Block Courage Award in 2009?

    A)   Bart Scott
    B)   Nick Mangold
    C)   David Harris
    D)   Brad Smith

26) New York has an all-time winning record against every AFC East opponent.

    A)   True
    B)   False

27) Which of the following Jets defensive linemen was not a member of the New York Sack Exchange?

    A)   Mark Gastineau
    B)   Marty Lyons
    C)   Joe Klecko
    D)   Gerry Philbin

28) Who was the most recent Jet to lead the NFL in yards per kickoff return?

    A)   Ron Carpenter
    B)   Justin Miller
    C)   Booby Humphrey
    D)   Leon Washington

29) Which decade did New York have its lowest winning percentage?

    A)  1970s
    B)  1980s
    C)  1990s
    D)  2000s

30) The Jets were penalized for greater than 1,000 yards in 2009 (including the postseason).

    A)  True
    B)  False

31) Who gave former Jets running back Curtis Martin the nickname Curtis "My Favorite" Martin?

    A)  Jim Nantz
    B)  Dick Enberg
    C)  Chris Berman
    D)  Pat Summerall

32) When was the last time the Jets rushed for over 300 yards as a team?

    A)  1995
    B)  2002
    C)  2004
    D)  2009

33) When was the last season the Jets gave up a safety?

    A) 1997
    B) 2001
    C) 2004
    D) 2008

34) What is the largest defeat New York ever suffered in a postseason game?

    A) 18 points
    B) 21 points
    C) 24 points
    D) 31 points

35) What is New York's record for consecutive regular-season wins?

    A) 5
    B) 6
    C) 8
    D) 9

36) Since 1970, has New York ever led the league in passing offense or total offense?

    A) Yes
    B) No

37) How many stripes are on the Jets' helmets?

   A) 0
   B) 1
   C) 2
   D) 3

38) When was the last season the Jets allowed a two-point conversion?

   A) 2004
   B) 2005
   C) 2007
   D) 2008

39) Who holds New York's record for most consecutive seasons leading the team in total tackles?

   A) Mo Lewis
   B) Victor Green
   C) Kyle Clifton
   D) Sam Cowart

40) Do the Jets have a regular-season winning record against the previous year's Super Bowl Champion?

   A) Yes
   B) No

41) What is the largest crowd to ever attend a Jets home game?

    A) 78,254
    B) 78,809
    C) 79,469
    D) 85,707

42) What season did the Jets play in their only American Bowl game?

    A) 1995
    B) 1998
    C) 2000
    D) 2003

43) Which of the following Jets quarterbacks never had a 400-yard passing game?

    A) Boomer Esiason
    B) Glenn Foley
    C) Richard Todd
    D) Vinny Testaverde

44) What was the highest winning percentage of a New York head coach who lasted one season or less?

    A) .357
    B) .406
    C) .481
    D) .563

45) Who was the most recent opponent New York shut out?

    A)   Tampa Bay Buccaneers
    B)   Cincinnati Bengals
    C)   Oakland Raiders
    D)   Pittsburgh Steelers

46) Who holds New York's record for most points scored in a single season?

    A)   Jay Feely
    B)   Pat Leahy
    C)   Jim Turner
    D)   Bobby Howfield

47) Against which team did New York's Mark Sanchez have the highest passer rating in 2009?

    A)   Oakland Raiders
    B)   Houston Texans
    C)   Miami Dolphins
    D)   Atlanta Falcons

48) What is New York's record for most consecutive wins at home?

    A)   6
    B)   8
    C)   10
    D)   11

49) Who holds New York's career postseason rushing yards record?

    A) Curtis Martin
    B) Matt Snell
    C) LaMont Jordan
    D) Freeman McNeil

50) What type of surface did the Jets play on in Giants Stadium?

    A) AstroTurf
    B) Natural Grass
    C) FieldTurf
    D) Matrix Artificial Turf

On Nov. 17, 1968, there was a game between the Jets and Raiders that has become known as "The Heidi Game". It is one of the most memorable regular-season games in pro football history. This is because of NBC's decision to cut to the start of a made-for-TV children's movie called "Heidi", with just 65 seconds left in the game. Both teams entered the game with 7-2 records, the Raiders were the defending AFL Champions and the Jets were led by star quarterback Joe Namath. The Jets had just taken the lead on a Jim Turner field goal, making the score 32-29. NBC was under contract with the movie's sponsor, Timex, to air the movie at exactly 7 o'clock. They cut away just after the Raiders took the ensuing kickoff at their own 23-yard line. While millions of football fans suddenly found themselves watching "Heidi", the Raiders scored two touchdowns in three plays to win the game 43-32. Due to this, the NFL's television contracts have been changed so that all games are shown in their entirety, regardless of length. Six weeks after The Heidi Game, the Jets would come from behind to defeat the Raiders 27-23 in the 1968 AFL Championship game and go on to win Super Bowl III.

1) B – 1988 (The Jets tied the Chiefs [17-17] at home on Oct. 2, 1988.)

2) D – New England Patriots (New York lost to the Patriots by 17 points [14-31] in Week 11.)

3) B – 3 (Joe Namath [#12], Don Maynard [#13], and Joe Klecko [#73])

4) B – No (The most touchdowns in a game by a running back is three [Emerson Boozer three times; Kevin Long and Charles Martin two times each; and Billy Joe, Johnny Hector, and Thomas Jones once each].)

5) A – Jay Feely (Jay made 24 consecutive field goals from 2008-09 before missing a 44-yarder against the Bills, ending his record streak.)

6) C – Rex Ryan (In 2009, New York beat Houston [24-7] in Ryan's first official game. Jets head coaches are 8-9 in their first official games.)

7) A – 2 (The Jets appeared in the postseason two years in a row on four occasions [1968-69, 1981-82, 1985-86, and 2001-02].)

8) B – Weeb Ewbank (Inducted in the Class of 1978, Weeb is the only coach to win world championships in the AFL and the NFL [1958 and 1959 Baltimore Colts, and the 1968 Jets].)

9) D – Philadelphia Eagles (The Jets have an all-time record of 0-8 against the Eagles, for a .000 winning percentage.)

10) A – Yes (Bill coached the Patriots from 1993-96, compiling a 32-32 record.)

11) C – Don Maynard (Don was a First-Team All-Pro in 1969, but not in 1968.)

12) D – 2005 (NY's Ty Law intercepted Buffalo's Kelly Holcomb 3 times for 56 yards on Jan. 1, 2006.)

13) A – Rushing Touchdowns (Curtis led the NFL in rushing attempts [371], rushing yards [1,697], and touches [412]. He finished in a tie for eighth in rushing touchdowns with 12.)

14) B – Brian Hansen (Brian had a total of 4,090 yards on 99 punts in 1995.)

15) D – 2006 (The Jets were held scoreless by the Jaguars [0-41] on Oct. 8, 2006.)

16) A – True (Brett threw 22 interceptions as the Jets' quarterback in 2008.)

17) C – 8 (Erik McMillan in 1991 [2], 1989 [3], and 1988 [2]; Jerry Holmes in 1983 [2]; Bobby Jackson in 1982 [2]; Darrol Ray in 1980 [2]; Paul Crane in 1969 [2]; and Dick Christy in 1962 [2])

18) B – 1998 (Keyshawn Johnson [1,131 yards] and Wayne Chrebet [1,083 yards])

19) A – Joe Klecko (Joe recorded a full sack in 10 consecutive games in 1977-78 [last six games in 1977 and first four in 1978].)

20) D – Chad Pennington (Chad set the team record in 2002 with a passer rating of 104.2. He finished the season with 275 completions on 399 attempts [.689], 22 touchdowns, 6 INTs, and 3,120 yards.)

21) B – 17 (Starting with Sammy Baugh to Rex Ryan)

22) C – 27 points (The Jets beat the Dolphins by this margin twice, once at home in 2004 [41-14] and at Miami in 2007 [40-13].)

23) D – Herman Edwards (Herm went 39-41 from 2001-05 for a .488 winning percentage.)

24) A – Yes (The Jets have played the Houston Texans the fewest number of times [4].)

25) C – David Harris (This award is given to a player from each team who exemplifies and displays courage. The team voted to give the award to David for coming back from an injury in the 2008 season.)

26) B – False (The Jets have an all-time winning record against Miami [46-41-1, .528] and New England, [50-48-1, .510], but have a losing record against Buffalo [45-53, .459].)

27) D – Gerry Philbin (Gerry played for the Jets from 1964-72, before the New York Sack Exchange came into existence. The fourth member of this defensive line with the famous nickname from the 1980s was Abdul Salaam.)

28) B – Justin Miller (Justin led the league in 2006 with 1,304 yards on 46 returns for a 28.3 average.)

29) A – 1970s (The Jets went 53-91, for a .368 winning percentage.)

30) B – False (NY was penalized 108 times for 836 yards.)

31) C – Chris Berman (This nickname comes from Berman's unique play on words of a 1960s television show "My Favorite Martian".)

32) D – 2009 (The Jets rushed for over 300 yards against the Bills [318 yards] and the Raiders [316 yards], a team feat not accomplished since 1998.)

33) C – 2004 (Pat Williams of Buffalo tackled Curtis Martin in the end zone for a loss of a yard and a safety. The Jets lost 22-17 to the Bills on Nov. 7, 2004.)

34) B – 21 points (The Jets lost 16-37 to the Patriots in the 2006 AFC Wild Card game.)

35) D – 9 (The Jets won nine straight games during the 1986 season.)

36) A – Yes (New York led the league in passing offense in 1972 with 2,777 yards.)

37) C – 2 (The Jets have had two green stripes on their white helmets since 1998.)

38) D – 2008 (Jabar Gaffney caught a Matt Cassel pass for a two-point conversion in a Jets win against the Patriots on Nov. 13, 2008.)

39) C – Kyle Clifton (He led the Jets in total tackles from 1988-91.)

40) B – No (The Jets are 3-16 [.158] all-time against Super Bowl winners from the previous year.)

41) C – 79,469 (This record was set on Sept. 20, 1998, in a game against the Indianapolis Colts.)

42) D – 2003 (The Jets played the Buccaneers in the Tokyo Dome in Japan losing 14-30 on Aug. 2, 2003, in their final preseason game of that year.)

43) A – Boomer Esiason (Boomer's highest total was 382 yards against Miami in 1994.)

44) D – .563 (Al Groh coached the 2000 Jets to a 9-7 record.)

45) B – Cincinnati Bengals (The Jets beat the Bengals 37-0 in the last regular-season game of 2009.)

46) C – Jim Turner (Jim scored 145 points in 1968 on 34 FGs and 43 PATs.)

47) A – Oakland Raiders (Mark had a season high 107.0 passer rating on 9 of 16 passing for 143 yards, 1 touchdown, and no interceptions.)

48) B – 8 (New York won eight straight home games in 1998, which includes a 34-24 win over the Jacksonville Jaguars in the 1998 Divisional Championship game.)

49) D – Freeman McNeil (Freeman gained 633 yards on 150 carries in eight postseason games from 1981-91.)

50) C – FieldTurf (This artificial surface was installed in 2003.)

Note: All answers valid as of the end of the 2009 season, unless otherwise indicated in the question itself.

1) How many career touchdown passes did Joe Namath have for the Jets?

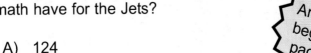

Answers begin on page 83

    A)  124
B)  141
C)  170
D)  203

2) What is the Jets' longest winning streak in the New York-Miami series?

    A)  7
B)  8
C)  10
D)  11

3) How many Jets have started in five or more Pro Bowls?

    A)  3
B)  4
C)  6
D)  9

4) New York has the all-time highest postseason winning percentage in the NFL.

    A)  True
B)  False

5) What is the nickname given to Jets superfan Ed Anzalone?

    A)   Chief Zee
    B)   Barrel Man
    C)   Crazy Eddie
    D)   Fireman Ed

6) How many times has New York played in the NFL Hall of Fame Game Series?

    A)   2
    B)   3
    C)   5
    D)   6

7) What year did the Jets finish the season with only one win?

    A)   1975
    B)   1977
    C)   1995
    D)   1996

8) How many Jets have been named Pro Bowl MVP?

    A)   1
    B)   2
    C)   3
    D)   5

9) How many touchdown drives of 80 or more yards did the Jets have in the 2009 regular season?

    A)  6
    B)  8
    C)  9
    D)  11

10) What are the most points ever scored by New York in a single game?

    A)  52
    B)  54
    C)  62
    D)  67

1) C – 170 (Namath is the Jets' all-time leader in career touchdown passes.)

2) B – 8 (New York won eight straight from 1966-69 and again from 1998-2001.)

3) C – 6 (Joe Namath [5], Larry Grantham [5], Mark Gastineau [5], Marvin Powell [5], Kevin Mawae [6], and Winston Hill [8])

4) B – False (New York is currently tied for 16th out of 32 NFL teams for all-time winning percentage [10-12, .455].)

5) D – Fireman Ed (New York City Fireman Ed Anzalone has been attending Jets home games since 1986, he leads fans in the famous chant "J-E-T-S".)

6) A – 2 (In 1977 the Jets lost to the Bears 20-6. In 1992 the Jets beat the Eagles 41-14.)

7) D – 1996 (The Jets were 1-15 under head coach Rich Kotite.)

8) B – 2 (Mark Gastineau [1985] and Keyshawn Johnson [1999])

9) A – 6 (The most 80-yard scoring drives came against the Texans [2].)

10) C – 62 (The Jets beat the Buccaneers 62-28 on Nov. 17, 1985.)

Note: All answers valid as of the end of the 2009 season, unless otherwise indicated in the question itself.

# Player / Team Score Sheet

Name:_____

| First Quarter | | | Second Quarter | | | Third Quarter | | | Fourth Quarter | | | Overtime Bonus | |
|---|---|---|---|---|---|---|---|---|---|---|---|---|---|
| 1 | 26 | | 1 | 26 | | 1 | 26 | | 1 | 26 | | 1 | |
| 2 | 27 | | 2 | 27 | | 2 | 27 | | 2 | 27 | | 2 | |
| 3 | 28 | | 3 | 28 | | 3 | 28 | | 3 | 28 | | 3 | |
| 4 | 29 | | 4 | 29 | | 4 | 29 | | 4 | 29 | | 4 | |
| 5 | 30 | | 5 | 30 | | 5 | 30 | | 5 | 30 | | 5 | |
| 6 | 31 | | 6 | 31 | | 6 | 31 | | 6 | 31 | | 6 | |
| 7 | 32 | | 7 | 32 | | 7 | 32 | | 7 | 32 | | 7 | |
| 8 | 33 | | 8 | 33 | | 8 | 33 | | 8 | 33 | | 8 | |
| 9 | 34 | | 9 | 34 | | 9 | 34 | | 9 | 34 | | 9 | |
| 10 | 35 | | 10 | 35 | | 10 | 35 | | 10 | 35 | | 10 | |
| 11 | 36 | | 11 | 36 | | 11 | 36 | | 11 | 36 | | | |
| 12 | 37 | | 12 | 37 | | 12 | 37 | | 12 | 37 | | | |
| 13 | 38 | | 13 | 38 | | 13 | 38 | | 13 | 38 | | | |
| 14 | 39 | | 14 | 39 | | 14 | 39 | | 14 | 39 | | | |
| 15 | 40 | | 15 | 40 | | 15 | 40 | | 15 | 40 | | | |
| 16 | 41 | | 16 | 41 | | 16 | 41 | | 16 | 41 | | | |
| 17 | 42 | | 17 | 42 | | 17 | 42 | | 17 | 42 | | | |
| 18 | 43 | | 18 | 43 | | 18 | 43 | | 18 | 43 | | | |
| 19 | 44 | | 19 | 44 | | 19 | 44 | | 19 | 44 | | | |
| 20 | 45 | | 20 | 45 | | 20 | 45 | | 20 | 45 | | | |
| 21 | 46 | | 21 | 46 | | 21 | 46 | | 21 | 46 | | | |
| 22 | 47 | | 22 | 47 | | 22 | 47 | | 22 | 47 | | | |
| 23 | 48 | | 23 | 48 | | 23 | 48 | | 23 | 48 | | | |
| 24 | 49 | | 24 | 49 | | 24 | 49 | | 24 | 49 | | | |
| 25 | 50 | | 25 | 50 | | 25 | 50 | | 25 | 50 | | | |
| ___ x 1 =____ | | | ___ x 2 =____ | | | ___ x 3 =____ | | | ___ x 4 =____ | | | ___ x 4 =____ | |

Multiply total number correct by point value/quarter to calculate totals for each quarter.

Add total of all quarters below.

**Total Points:**_____

Thank you for playing *Jetsology Trivia Challenge*.

**Additional score sheets are available at:**
**www.TriviaGameBooks.com**

# Player / Team Score Sheet

Name:_____

| First Quarter | | Second Quarter | | Third Quarter | | Fourth Quarter | | Overtime Bonus | |
|---|---|---|---|---|---|---|---|---|---|
| 1 | 26 | 1 | 26 | 1 | 26 | 1 | 26 | 1 | |
| 2 | 27 | 2 | 27 | 2 | 27 | 2 | 27 | 2 | |
| 3 | 28 | 3 | 28 | 3 | 28 | 3 | 28 | 3 | |
| 4 | 29 | 4 | 29 | 4 | 29 | 4 | 29 | 4 | |
| 5 | 30 | 5 | 30 | 5 | 30 | 5 | 30 | 5 | |
| 6 | 31 | 6 | 31 | 6 | 31 | 6 | 31 | 6 | |
| 7 | 32 | 7 | 32 | 7 | 32 | 7 | 32 | 7 | |
| 8 | 33 | 8 | 33 | 8 | 33 | 8 | 33 | 8 | |
| 9 | 34 | 9 | 34 | 9 | 34 | 9 | 34 | 9 | |
| 10 | 35 | 10 | 35 | 10 | 35 | 10 | 35 | 10 | |
| 11 | 36 | 11 | 36 | 11 | 36 | 11 | 36 | | |
| 12 | 37 | 12 | 37 | 12 | 37 | 12 | 37 | | |
| 13 | 38 | 13 | 38 | 13 | 38 | 13 | 38 | | |
| 14 | 39 | 14 | 39 | 14 | 39 | 14 | 39 | | |
| 15 | 40 | 15 | 40 | 15 | 40 | 15 | 40 | | |
| 16 | 41 | 16 | 41 | 16 | 41 | 16 | 41 | | |
| 17 | 42 | 17 | 42 | 17 | 42 | 17 | 42 | | |
| 18 | 43 | 18 | 43 | 18 | 43 | 18 | 43 | | |
| 19 | 44 | 19 | 44 | 19 | 44 | 19 | 44 | | |
| 20 | 45 | 20 | 45 | 20 | 45 | 20 | 45 | | |
| 21 | 46 | 21 | 46 | 21 | 46 | 21 | 46 | | |
| 22 | 47 | 22 | 47 | 22 | 47 | 22 | 47 | | |
| 23 | 48 | 23 | 48 | 23 | 48 | 23 | 48 | | |
| 24 | 49 | 24 | 49 | 24 | 49 | 24 | 49 | | |
| 25 | 50 | 25 | 50 | 25 | 50 | 25 | 50 | | |
| ___ x 1 = ___ | | ___ x 2 = ___ | | ___ x 3 = ___ | | ___ x 4 = ___ | | ___ x 4 = ___ | |

Multiply total number correct by point value/quarter to calculate totals for each quarter.

Add total of all quarters below.

## Total Points:_____

Thank you for playing *Jetsology Trivia Challenge*.

**Additional score sheets are available at:**
**www.TriviaGameBooks.com**